Mrs. GreenJeans

Works Out The Worries

(An Adult-Guided Workbook for Children)

Mrs. GreenJeans

Works Out The Worries

(An Adult-Guided Workbook for Children)

Ebony Jackson Brown MSW, LCSW

Copyright

Copyright © 2017 by Ebony Jackson Brown, MSW, LCSW. All rights reserved. This book or any portion thereof may not be reproduced or used in any manner whatsoever without the express written permission of Ebony Jackson Brown, MSW, LCSW except for the use of brief quotations in a book review.

Printed in the United States of America

First Printing, 2017

ISBN-13: 978-0-9909919-2-2

ISBN10: 099099192x

References

Diagnostic and statistical manual of mental disorders fifth edition DSM-5 American psychiatric association

Greenberger, P. D., & Padesky, P. C. (1995). Mind Over Mood: Change How You Feel by Changing the Way You Think. New York: The Guilford Press.

The Butterfly Typeface Publishing
PO BOX 56193
Little Rock Arkansas 72215

Disclaimer

The *Mrs. GreenJeans* series is designed to provide information about the subject matter covered. This book is not a replacement for therapeutic services and should not be used to assist with diagnosis.

Clinicians should refer to the DSM-5 for diagnosis criteria. It is sold with the understanding that this book is not a replacement for professional services. The publisher and author are not engaged in rendering therapeutic professional services through the use of this literature. If therapeutic assistance is required, the services of a competent and qualified professional should be sought.

The information provided should not be considered as all inclusive. Therefore, this text should be used only as an example and entertainment, not as the ultimate source of therapeutic information. Furthermore, these books contain information on therapeutic information and techniques only up to the printing date.

The purpose of these book is to educate and to entertain.

The author and Butterfly Typeface Publishing shall have neither liability nor responsibility to any person or entity with respect to any loss or damage caused or alleged to be caused directly or indirectly by the information contained in these books.

For those who struggle with anxiety.

"Deep Breathing; Challenging Your Thoughts."
-Mrs. GreenJeans

To my loving and supportive husband,
as well as our four children.

Look for other books in the

Mrs. GreenJeans

Series

Vocabulary

Depicts ⟶ Show or represent

Validity ⟶ Factually

Diversion ⟶ Turn from the course

Irrational ⟶ Not reasonable

Overwhelmed ⟶ Completely defeated, engulfed

Table of Contents

Vocabulary 13

You 18

Feeling Anxious 19

Anxiety 21

Physical Reaction 23

Therapy 27

Imagery 28

Problem Solving 30

Challenging Thoughts 32

Diversion 35

Worry 37

Your Support Group 39

A Letter to Self 42

About the Author 49

You

My Name is Willow.
You've just finish reading my story,
now I would like to know all about you.
Let's get to know each other beginning with your name.
Write your full name in the space below.

_____

Feeling Anxious

In my story, there were many situations that made me feel anxious. Feelings are an emotional state that directly influences the way we respond to others, and the world around us. The way we feel can influence our ability to learn and interact with others. Now that you have read all about me, I would like to know who you are. In the space below draw a picture that depicts who you are or write five words that best describe you.

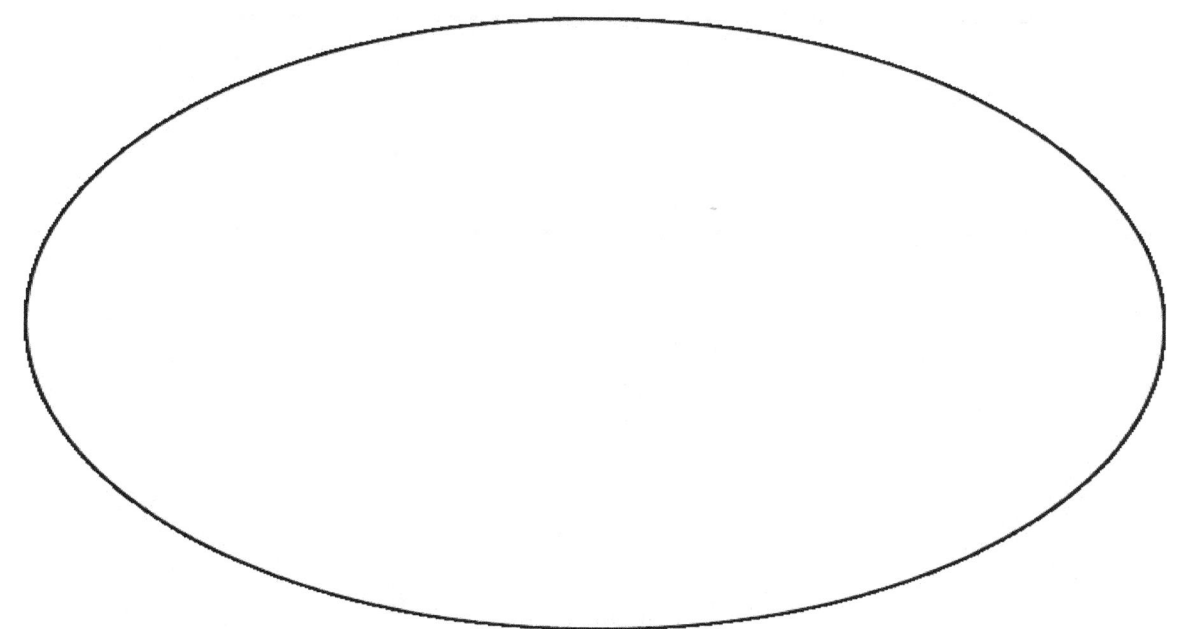

Anxiety

If you don't know by now, I will tell you that I have anxiety which causes me to worry more than most people. Anxiety is a feeling that causes one to worry, feel nervous, or fearful about an unclear outcome. In my story, I felt nervous about people staring at me, facing Craig the bully, and many other situations.

In the space provided below, draw or list situations that cause you to feel worried, nervous or fearful.

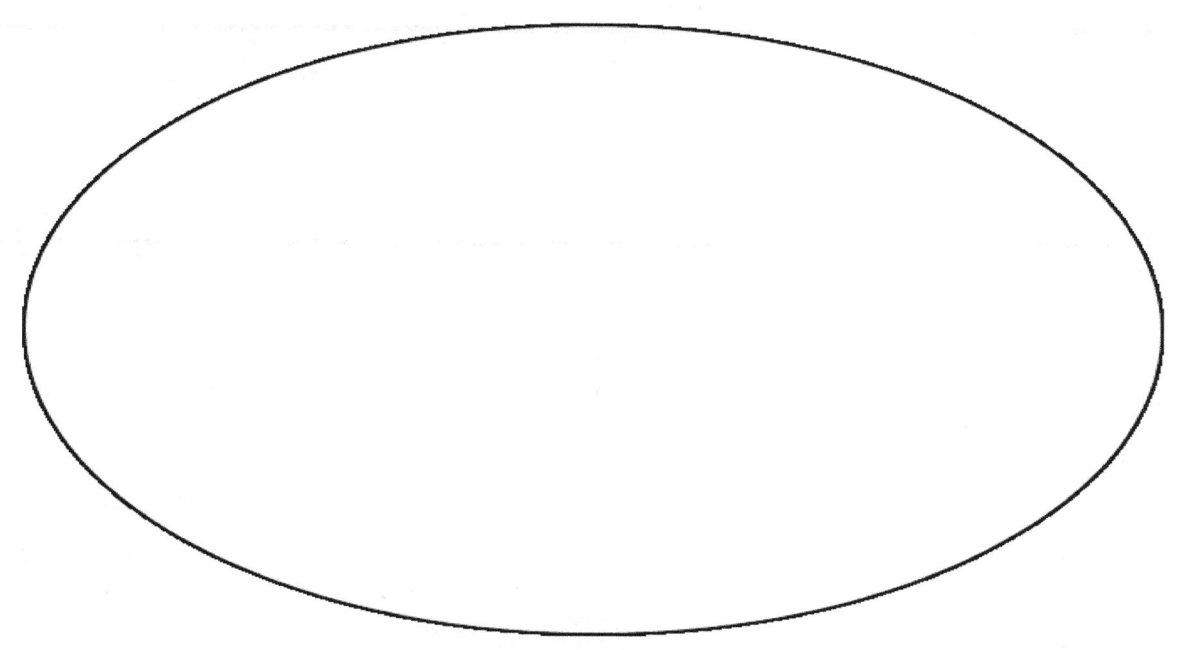

Physical Reaction

In my story my anxiety caused my body to respond in different ways, sweat rolled down my back when I became nervous, and my palms began to sweat as I reached to shake Mrs. GreenJeans hand. Anxiety can cause a physical reaction that happens when we feel fearful of the unknown. What happens when you feel worried or fearful?

Draw or write your response in the spaces provided below.

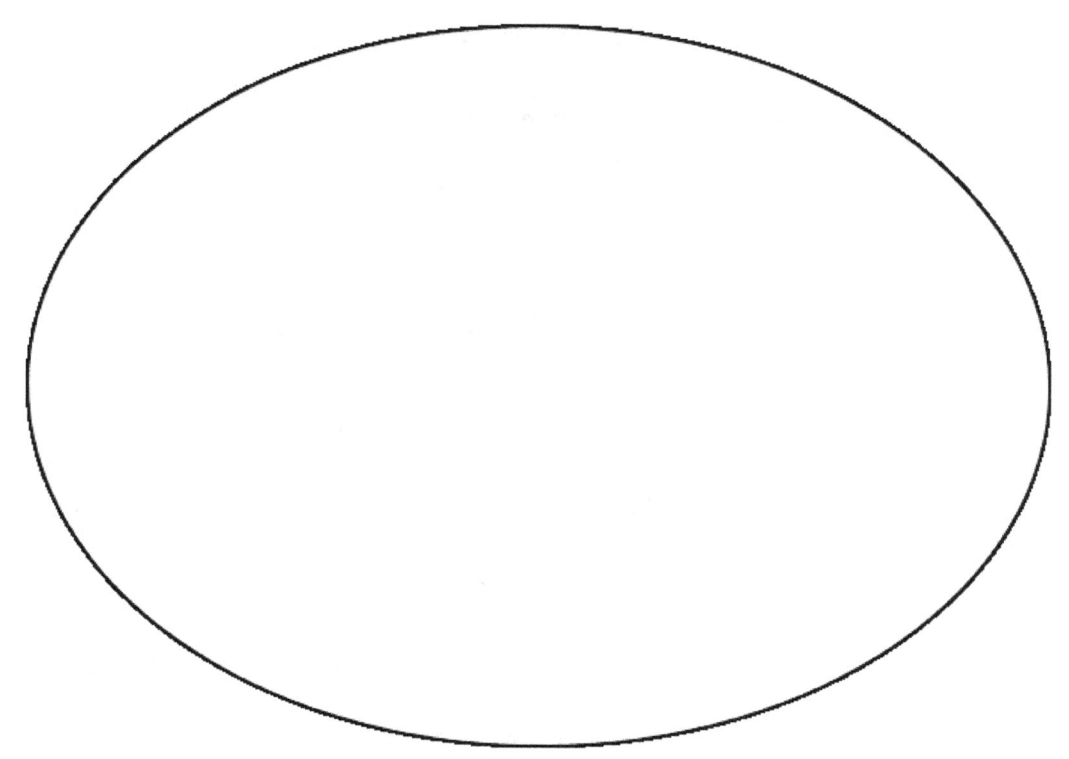

Some situations cause an increased anxiety response; you may be more fearful of one situation verses another situation.

More Fearful

For example, I was more fearful of meeting Craig at the flag pole after school than I was of shaking Mrs. GreenJeans' hand.

In the space provided below, list what makes you most worried then use the graph to indicate the intensity.

I feel most worried when the following occurs:

I would rate my anxiety level as:

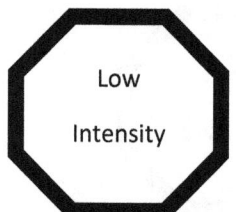 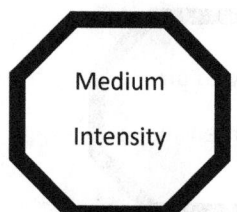 

Some situations cause an increased anxiety response; you may be more fearful of one situation verses another situation.

Least Fearful

For example, I was more fearful of meeting Craig at the flag pole after school than I was of shaking Mrs. GreenJeans' hand.

In the spaces provided below, list what makes you least worried, then use the graph to indicate the intensity.

I feel least fearful when this occurs, yet still fearful:

I would rate my anxiety level as:

Therapy

Mrs. GreenJeans is my therapist. A therapist is a skilled individual taught to help a person cope with emotional and behavioral issues. Mrs. GreenJeans taught me a relaxation technique called deep breathing. Deep breathing will help decrease your anxiety. You can practice deep breathing with your therapist, your parent, or even on your own. To practice deep breathing, inhale slowly and exhale slowly. Counting to five maybe helpful while you are taking slow deep breaths.

Let's pause and take a minute to practice.

                Inhale slowly counting

        one .... two.... three.... Four .... Five

                Exhale slowly counting

        five .... four ......there.... two ....one

Imagery

Mrs. GreenJeans taught me another helpful skill called imagery. Imagery is when you imagine a relaxing place in your mind to decrease your anxiety. Let's practice!

You are sitting in the movie theater watching your favorite movie. The theater is quiet; you hear nothing but the sound of your favorite feature movie. Your seat is covered in soft leather and slightly laid back. You have a large bucket of popcorn and your favorite soft drink.

You are riding on your favorite bike trail during the Fall. The trees have turned bright yellow, red, orange and some are still green. You hear the leaves crackling under your bicycle wheel as you ride. While you are riding, you see a squirrel running up the tree in the distance. You are riding further and faster, you feel the wind on your face.

You are at home in your room lying back in your bed. You have your headphones in listening to your favorite music. Your room is quiet and the rooms temperature is just right. You close your eyes and drift off to sleep.

In the space provided below, write about three of your favorite imagery scene or draw a picture.

_____

_____

_____

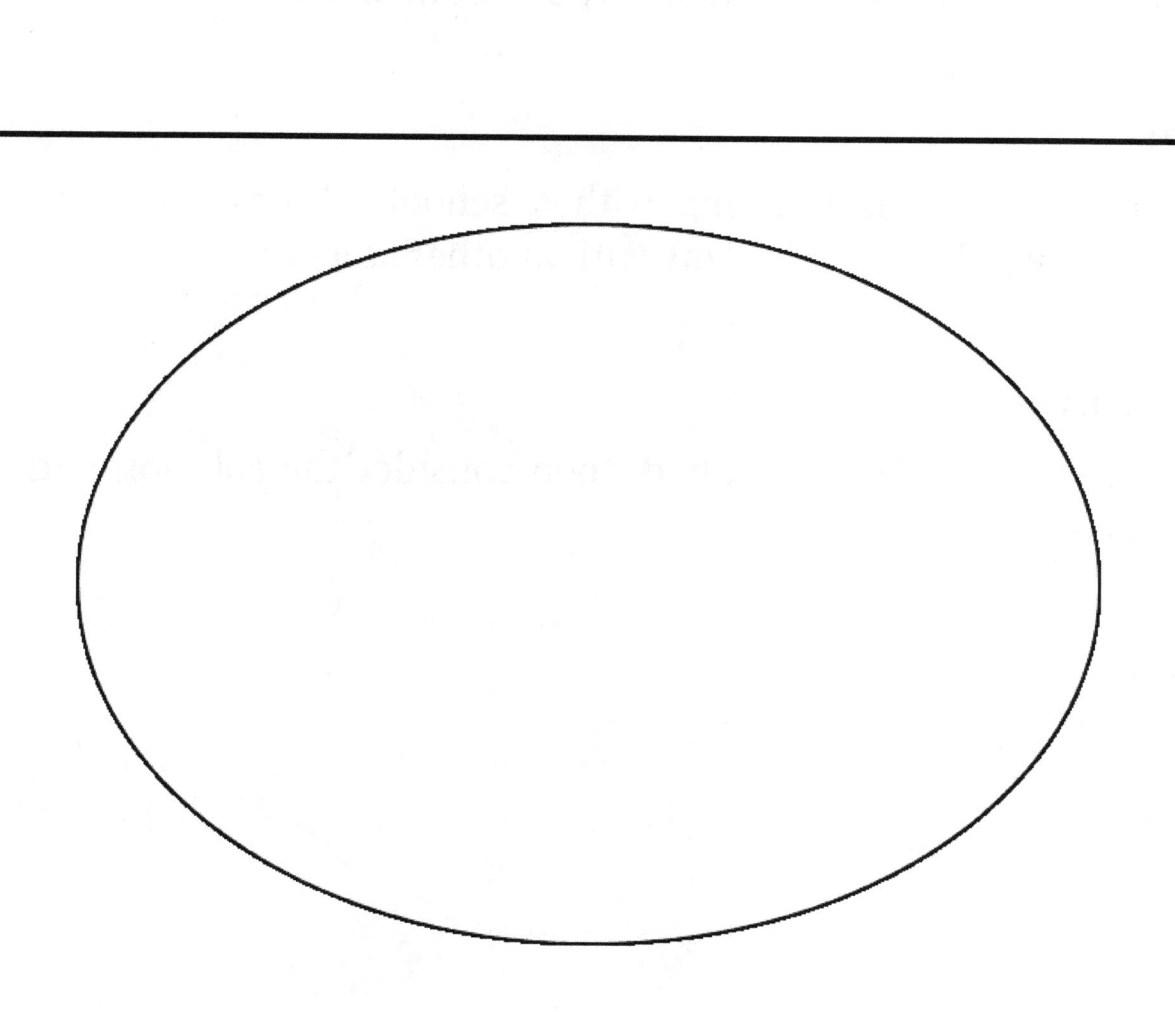

Problem Solving

Mrs. GreenJeans taught me how to use problem solving skills. The first step is identifying the problem. The next step is coming up with a solution to the problem. The last step is to act assertively to resolve the problem. Let's practice below.

Problem:

I'm afraid that Craig was angry at me for winning class representative. He told me he was going to meet me by the flag pole after school. I'm afraid that he may become violent.

Solution:

The appropriate thing to do is to notify a staff member in the school.

Action:

I will leave out of the building with a school administrator. I will not respond to Craig. I will walk home with another student.

Your Turn:

Try to think of a problem you had, then consider the solution and list the action taken.

Problem:

Solution:

Action:

Let's try again.

Problem:

Willow became overwhelmed with anxiety when her teacher, Ms. Sourbottoms searched the classroom for someone to answer the math equation.

Solution:

Prepare to answer the question by finding the answer.

Action:

Take slow deep breaths then answer the question.

Your turn.

Try to think of a problem you had, then consider the solution and list the action taken.

Problem:

Solution:

Action:

Challenging Thoughts

Mrs. GreenJeans also taught me to challenge my thoughts. Sometimes I worry about things that have no validity.

For example

I thought my classmates starred at me because they didn't like me when they really admire me for my thoughtfulness and kindness. I was elected classroom representative, I couldn't believe it!

You can challenge your thoughts by asking yourself a few questions such as:

1. What evidence do you have to support your thought?
2. Are you catastrophizing (blowing things out of proportion)?
3. Ask yourself if you could be wrong.

After you have challenged your thoughts, try to think of an alternative positive rational thought.

For Example

Irrational thought:

The girls in my classroom are staring at me because I am wearing old sneakers and jeans from last year.

Challenge question:

How would they know that these are the same jeans and sneakers from last year?

Alternative positive thought:

Perhaps they are admiring my sneakers and jeans because they are different.

Let's practice challenging our thoughts below.

Irrational thought:

Challenge question:

Alternative positive thought:

Let's practice challenging our thoughts below.

Irrational thought:

Challenge question:

Alternative positive thought:

Diversion

Diversion is another technique I use to divert my mind from worrying. You can do this too by finding things to do when the worry ensues such as:

Puzzles, crossword, coloring, board games, cards, swimming, biking, or watching a movie. What kind of fun things do you like to do that may divert your mind from worrying.

Draw a picture or list them below.

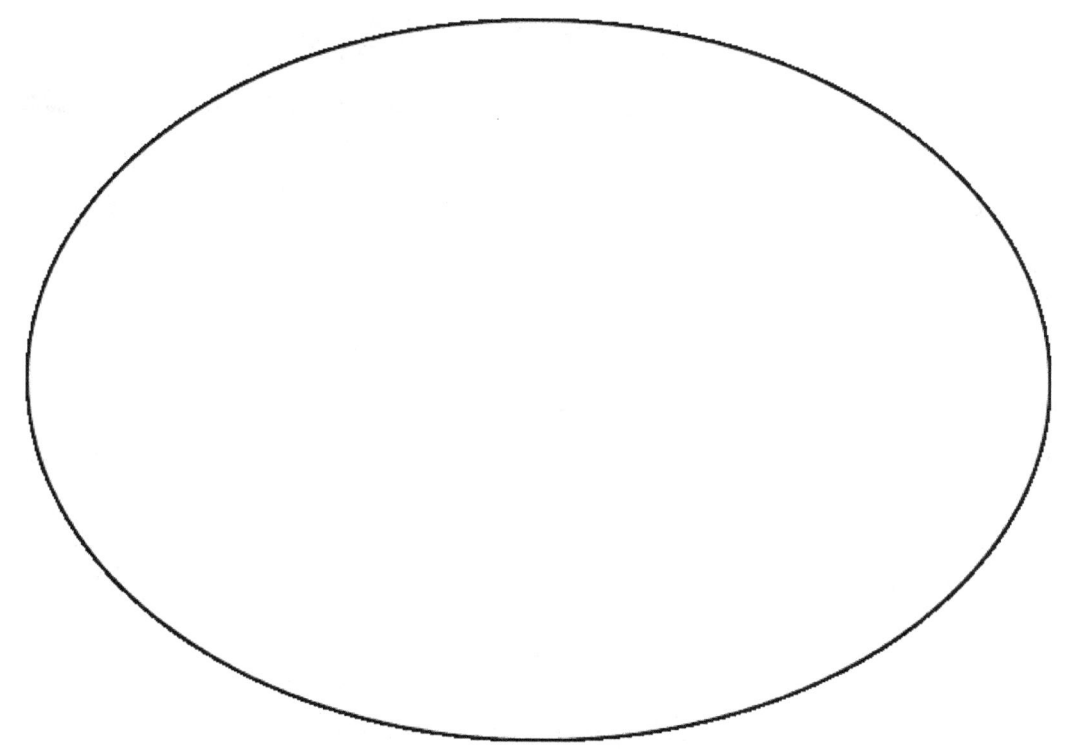

Worry

Worry can distract you from engaging in day to day task. When you are worried, your mind is not focused on what it should be, it's focused on what you are worried about.

When you are distracted with worry, you might not complete work, or pay attention to the work you are doing, you may even become forgetful. It's best to pick a time and place to work out your worries so that you can go about your day without worrying.

For example

I choose to work through my worries at bed time.

Tell me about the place and time you choose to work out your worries in the space provided below.

Your Support Group

Talking with friends you trust rather than keeping your feelings bottled up inside can help you work through your worry.

In my story, Violet and I are good friends. Violet is someone I can trust and share my feelings with.

Opening up about your feelings helps you feel less alone. In the space below, draw a picture or tell me about a time when you did tell someone how you felt.

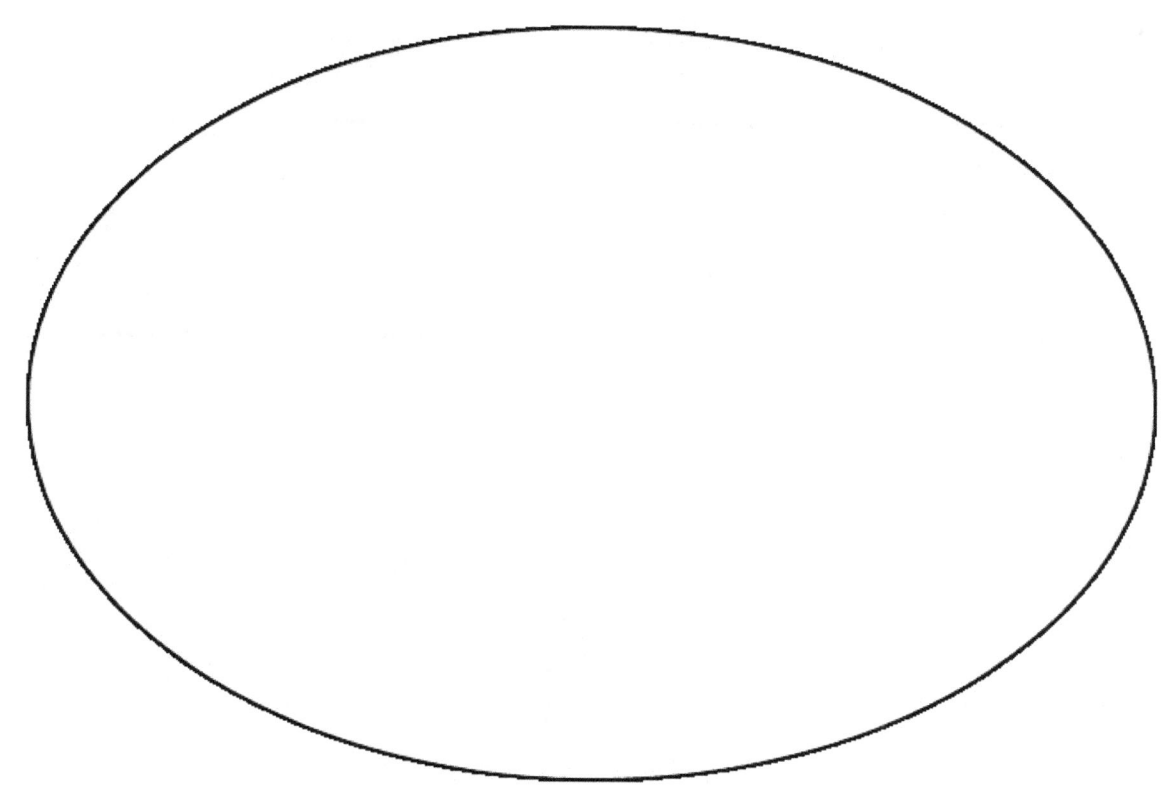

In Control of Me

In the story, *Mrs. GreenJeans Works Out The Worries*, we learn how unproductive worrying can be.

What this means is ...

Worrying about what people think and situations that may NEVER become a reality is a waste of time. Instead of worrying, use techniques to help control your anxiety such as deep breathing, imagery, problem solving, diversion, and challenging your thoughts to help you cope with your anxiety.

A letter to self

Finally, write a letter to yourself. Discuss what you have been worried about and which skill you plan to use to cope with your worry.

Dear self,

"You *can* control how you feel, Willow."
Mrs. GreenJeans

#ICOM

In Control of Me

About the Author

Author Ebony Jackson Brown is a retired Air Force wife who began her career as a childcare provider for military families during her husband's career in 1995.

She later decided she wanted to care for military personnel and families in a different capacity and sought an education in social work. Ebony graduated with a bachelor's degree from Methodist University in the field of social work. Subsequently Ebony graduated from the University of Southern California earning a Master of Social Work Degree, with a concentration in mental health and military social work.

The series, *Mrs. GreenJeans,* highlights diversity as mental illness is not discriminatory among races, ethnicities, or culture. The books are a representation of the capacity to which therapists affect change and growth in individuals and highlights the importance of therapy in our society. Therapists are professionals whom individuals should seek for direction and support while attempting to navigate life's problematic circumstances and situations.

The goal of the *Mrs. GreenJeans* series (storybooks, workbooks, and activity books) is to combat the stigma of mental health services so that seeking and engaging in mental health services is normalized.

Ebony Jackson Brown continues to provide care to military personnel and their families as a licensed clinical social worker. She and her husband of 26 years reside in North Carolina with their four children.

Tops of The Trees Books

An imprint of Butterfly Typeface Publishing

WWW.BUTTERFLYTYPEFACE.COM

www.ingramcontent.com/pod-product-compliance
Lightning Source LLC
Chambersburg PA
CBHW081502040426
42446CB00016B/3357